Color Me Purple

GAIL EASLING

COLOR ME PURPLE

Published by:
Quest Publications
6-176 Henry Street
Brantford, Ontario,
N3S 5C8, Canada
Website: *http://www.questpub.questforgod.org*
Email: *questpublications@outlook.com.*

Cover design and interior formatting by *Quest Publications*

ISBN-13: 978-1-988439-06-8

DEDICATION

Dedicated to my Creator,
mentor and inspiration

and to my grandchildren

and the children
around the world.

May you too experience the joy of walking
close to Him!

"Color me purple,

Color me red,

Color me bright

as I jump out of bed!

"What is that green thing?

Tell me quick!

What is that green thing

that I get to pick?"

Like straight little soldiers all in a row,

Photo © Marie Iannotti

Just watch the asparagus starting to grow.

Pea popping goodness,
pea popping fun,

"See all the green veggies
out in the sun!"

"Zucchini and green beans,
celery and peas,

There's even more green things under
the leaves.

Kiwi and basil, broccoli too

"I just touched a squash with the end of my shoe."

"Having a garden

is a delight to my eyes,

There's always
something growing

under bright blue skies!"

"Oh, what is that orange thing

that's getting so big?"

"And look!

Over here I see a new fig!"

"I'm so excited,

just look at me run!

Playing outdoors in the sunshine is fun!"

"Look mamma,

what is this I see?"

"Oh sweetheart,

it's our helpers,
the honey bees."

"Momma,

what is that I hear and feel?"

"It's just a little rain drop

and a mighty thunder peal."

"It's starting to rain,

now watch our garden grow,

And oh how I like squishy mud

oozing out through my toes."

"I've been very busy with

my hand rake and hoe,

Now *I* need some water

to help me to grow."

"The sunshine and work has tuckered me out,

Now I need some rest, if I'm going to sprout."

"With all the running and hoeing I've done,

I'll go eat my lunch and then to my bed I will run."

"I'm so exhausted,
I'll take a quick nap,

But first will you read me a story, while
I sit on your lap?"

ACKNOWLEDGMENT

A special thank you to

MARIE IANNOTTI

Gardening Expert & Author of
The Beginner's Guide to Growing Heirloom Vegetables: The 100 Easiest-
to-Grow, Tastiest Vegetables for Your Garden
(http://www.amazon.com/Marie-Iannotti/e/B0050PIEPI)

For sharing her practical insights and her joy for gardening.

&

DIANA STOLL

for allowing the use of her photo of strawberries
Website: http://gardenwithdiana.com

www.ingramcontent.com/pod-product-compliance
Lightning Source LLC
Chambersburg PA
CBHW041554040426
42447CB00002B/178